A Biome of the World: The Taiga

by Carol Talley

Scott Foresman
is an imprint of

PEARSON

Glenview, Illinois • Boston, Massachusetts • Chandler, Arizona
Upper Saddle River, New Jersey

Every effort has been made to secure permission and provide appropriate credit for photographic material. The publisher deeply regrets any omission and pledges to correct errors called to its attention in subsequent editions.

Unless otherwise acknowledged, all photographs are the property of Scott Foresman, a division of Pearson Education.

Photo locators denoted as follows: Top (T), Center (C), Bottom (B), Left (L), Right (R), Background (Bkgd)

4 Hans Strand/Getty Images; 6 Bryan and Cherry Alexander/Photo Researchers, Inc.; 8 Simon Fraser/Photo Researchers, Inc.; 10 Hush Rose/Visuals Unlimited; 15 Niall Benvie/Nature Picture Library; 17 Joseph Van OS/Getty Images; 18 Thomas and Pat Leeson/Photo Researchers, Inc.; 19 Lynn M. Stone/Nature Picture Library; 20 (T) Joe McDonald/Corbis, (B) Steve Kaufman/Corbis; 21 (BL) Layne Kennedy/Corbis, Corbis; 22 Farrell Grehan/Photo Researchers, Inc.;

ISBN 13: 978-0-328-52582-9
ISBN 10:   0-328-52582-0

Copyright © by Pearson Education, Inc., or its affiliates. All rights reserved.
Printed in the United States of America. This publication is protected by copyright, and permission should be obtained from the publisher prior to any prohibited reproduction, storage in a retrieval system, or transmission in any form or by any means, electronic, mechanical, photocopying, recording, or likewise. For information regarding permissions, write to Pearson Curriculum Rights & Permissions, One Lake Street, Upper Saddle River, New Jersey 07458.

Pearson® is a trademark, in the U.S. and/or in other countries, of Pearson plc or its affiliates.

Scott Foresman® is a trademark, in the U.S. and/or in other countries, of Pearson Education, Inc., or its affiliates.

3 4 5 6 7   V0N4   17 16 15 14 13 12 11 10

TABLE OF CONTENTS

CHAPTER 1 — 4
A World of Biomes

CHAPTER 2 — 6
The Climate of the Taiga

CHAPTER 3 — 8
Taiga Soil and Land

CHAPTER 4 — 10
Plants of the Taiga

CHAPTER 5 — 15
Animal Survival Tactics

CHAPTER 6 — 21
The People of the Taiga

Glossary — 24

Chapter 1 A World of Biomes

The taiga is a band of forests that lies just below the Arctic Circle. It is a large land biome that reaches around the world. In North America, it stretches from the island of Newfoundland, westward across Canada, and up through Alaska. It also cuts a wide path across parts of northern Japan, China, Mongolia, and most of Siberia. It continues through Russia and over the European countries of Finland, Sweden, and Norway, finishing in Scotland.

A biome is a major region of the Earth with a particular climate, a particular kind of land and soil, and a community of plants and animals that are adapted to living in that particular place. Examples of biomes are a desert and the ocean.

Scientists don't always agree on the number of biomes on Earth, on their exact borders, or even on the names of the biomes. *Taiga* is a Russian word that means "swamp forest," which is a good description of the taiga. Other names that some scientists use for the taiga are the boreal forest and the northern coniferous forest.

The green band shows the location of the taiga biome.

4

The word *boreal* means "northern." (Boreas was the Greek god of the north wind.) The word *coniferous* means "cone-bearing," which describes most of the trees in the taiga. Conifers are trees that produce their seeds in cones instead of in flowers.

To get a closer look at the taiga, it might be a good idea to hop aboard a single-engine bush plane. Whether you take off from an outpost in Siberia or a short runway in Canada, you will see pretty much the same thing—mile after mile of spruce, pine, fir, or larch trees beneath the plane, stretching as far as you can see in every direction. If it is winter, the taiga will be blanketed in snow and ice. If it is summer, your eye may catch the sparkle of a lake or river here and there among the trees. You may see a moose grazing at the water's edge, or a flock of birds settling into the treetops. But otherwise, the view will hardly change, even if you fly for hours and for hundreds of miles.

What conditions create the taiga world you see from your airplane?

Chapter 2 The Climate of the Taiga

Each type of biome develops in a certain type of climate. A climate is determined by the average weather conditions in an area over a long period of time. These weather conditions include the amount of precipitation (rain and snow) each year, temperature, sunlight, seasons, and wind.

The taiga's climate is unique. The winters are long and bitterly cold. For six months or more the temperature stays below freezing. At times the temperature **registers** at about −50°F and stays there for days. Even on the warmest winter days, the temperature does not rise above 30°F.

The coldest temperature ever registered in the northern hemisphere was in the taiga region: −90°F in the town of Verkhoyansk, in Siberia.

    Winter precipitation falls in the form of snow. Because of the constant freezing temperatures, the snow does not melt. All the water in the snow, in the ground, and in the lakes and rivers is frozen.

    Spring passes quickly in the taiga, followed by a short, wet summer with only about three months of frost-free days. Even in the warmest month of the summer, the average temperature is about 50°F, and the temperature seldom goes above 70°F. The growing season is very short. Plants and animals must take advantage of the sun and warmth while they can. Then, with barely a trace of autumn, the fierce winter returns.

Chapter 3 Taiga Soil and Land

What's beneath the surface is also important in the taiga. Many thousands of years ago, glaciers covered the regions of Earth that are now the taiga. When the glaciers receded at the end of the last ice age, they scraped the land and made deep cuts in the rocky surface. These gouged-out places filled with water and formed the lakes, rivers, and bogs of the taiga.

A bog is formed when soil, dead plants, and conifer needles build up in still lake waters. The plant materials decay very slowly in the cold water. Over time, they become a spongy mat. The bogs eventually fill up and become dry enough for larger plants. It is just a matter of time before conifer trees grow where the lake once was.

The soil that has formed in the taiga is not an inviting home for most plants. The ground beneath the trees in a warm southern forest is full of decaying plant and animal material. Push aside the leaves on the ground and you will find dark, rich soil.

But because of the cold climate in the taiga, and because conifer needles decompose slowly, soil forms slowly. Deep layers of undecayed vegetation pile up on the forest floor. If you push aside the layers, you will find a thin layer of soil that looks as gray as ashes.

If you go a little deeper into the soil of the taiga, you will find another obstacle to plant growth. Much of the taiga grows above a layer of permanently frozen ground called permafrost. A **hatchet** could not break this rock-hard layer. The roots of trees and other plants cannot force their way through it. Rain and melting snow cannot seep through the permafrost either. So the ground in the taiga stays soggy and soft.

Parts of the taiga where there is no permafrost–parts of Canada, for example–have a layer of rock not far beneath the soil. This rock also keeps water from draining away from the surface.

Can you think of plants and animals that might be able to survive the harsh conditions of the taiga?

Ponds like these eventually fill with debris and become part of the soil.

Chapter 4 Plants of the Taiga

Hardy Conifers

The taiga is crowded with trees. Most of the trees are conifers. They have small, needlelike leaves, and most—with the exception of larches—are evergreen. That means their leaves stay green all year long. Unlike deciduous trees, whose leaves fall off every autumn, a conifer's leaves will not fall until they are old. Spruce trees often keep their needles for fifteen years. Some other kinds of conifers only keep their leaves for two or three years. The most common evergreen conifers in the taiga are spruces, firs, and pines.

Conifers are the most common trees in the taiga. Here, pine trees end abruptly at the Alaskan tundra.

Pinecones of a spruce tree

Conifer trees can endure cold, snow, a lack of water in winter, and a short growing season in summer. Have you ever seen the branches of a tree break under the weight of a heavy load of snow? Most conifers have a spirelike shape, with a pointed top and sloping sides, that minimizes this kind of damage. This shape allows the snow to slide right off the flexible branches of the tree.

The needlelike leaves of the conifers also help protect them from winter damage. The narrowness of the leaves reduces the surface area from which water may be lost through evaporation. This is especially important during the winter, when the roots of the trees are unable to get water from the ground. Conifer needles also have a thick, waxy outer coating that helps hold water in.

When spring finally arrives and temperatures become warmer, conifers are able to begin growing immediately to take full advantage of the short growing season. Because conifer trees have shallow roots, growing out to the sides of the tree instead of deep down into the ground, they are able to begin absorbing water as soon as the upper layer of the soil begins to thaw.

Deciduous trees must produce new leaves in the spring before they can begin using sunlight to manufacture food. Both conifers and deciduous trees manufacture food through the process of photosynthesis. The green color of a leaf is caused by a chemical called chlorophyll. It absorbs sunlight and turns it into food for the tree.

Because most conifers are evergreen and do not shed their leaves each year, they do not have to waste precious time growing new needles each spring. They can get right to work on the first spring day, making food and growing.

The dark green color of spruce and fir needles also helps the trees absorb more nutrients from the sun's rays and helps these trees begin making food in the spring.

In the coldest, harshest regions of the taiga, especially in northern Siberia, even the hardy evergreen needles cannot survive. In these regions another conifer takes over–the larch. Unlike spruces, firs, and pines, the larch is a deciduous conifer. It sheds its needles in winter, reducing water loss and keeping frost damage to a minimum. Larches grow farther north than any other tree.

Black spruce, dwarf birch, and willow mix together in this region of the taiga in Alaska.

Other Trees of the Taiga

The conifers–spruces, firs, pines, and larches–dominate the taiga, but a few deciduous trees manage to survive in this climate as well. Deciduous trees have broad rather than needlelike leaves and are common in areas that have been cleared by fire, disease, wind, or logging. They can also be found along the edges of ponds, bogs, and rivers. Aspen, birch, alder, poplar, and willow are five deciduous trees that are found in the taiga.

Taiga Trees Are Not Alone

The ground in the taiga does not make an inviting home for other plants. The deep blanket of fallen evergreen needles makes it hard for small plants and shrubs to get a foothold. The roots of the conifers take the water and nutrients from the soil below, and their dark green branches block out the sun overhead.

However, a few hardy plants are able to take hold in the partially frozen ground. In summer, ferns, mosses, and lichens are able to grow on the moist forest floor under the taiga's trees and sometimes on the trees themselves. In places where sunlight is able to break through, blueberries, highbush cranberries, and other shrubs grow in masses. Grasslike sedges, willows, and other water-loving plants grow in wet areas such as the taiga bogs.

Mushrooms are also able to grow in the taiga. These fungi live off of the decaying material on the forest floor.

Fire in the Taiga

Fires are common in the taiga, often started when lightning **ignites** dry conifer needles. Fire is a normal part of a forest's life, allowing it to renew itself. Many trees and other plants are killed, but where hot ashes once **smoldered,** new vegetation soon appears. Some conifers benefit from fires. For example, some pinecones will open and release their seeds only when heated by a forest fire.

Chapter 5 Animal Survival Tactics

The taiga has fewer kinds of animals than forests located in warmer regions. Most are mammals, birds, and insects. Very few amphibians or reptiles live in the taiga.

Some of the more common mammals in the taiga are moose, caribou (reindeer), porcupines, gray wolves, snowshoe hares, red squirrels, and mice.

A few birds are year-round residents of the taiga– ruffed grouse, crossbills, gray and blue jays, nuthatches, woodpeckers, chickadees, and owls. Many other types of birds spend their winters in warmer climates and migrate north to the taiga for the spring and summer months.

A few taiga animals survive the winter by hibernating, living off the fat they have built up in their bodies during the summer. During hibernation, their pulse rate and breathing slow down, their body temperature is lowered close to freezing, and they become almost motionless.

Red squirrels are common animals in the taiga.

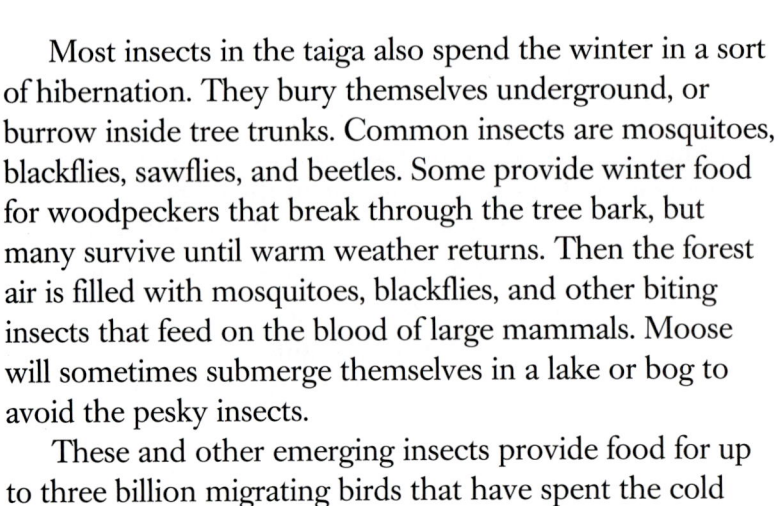

Most insects in the taiga also spend the winter in a sort of hibernation. They bury themselves underground, or burrow inside tree trunks. Common insects are mosquitoes, blackflies, sawflies, and beetles. Some provide winter food for woodpeckers that break through the tree bark, but many survive until warm weather returns. Then the forest air is filled with mosquitoes, blackflies, and other biting insects that feed on the blood of large mammals. Moose will sometimes submerge themselves in a lake or bog to avoid the pesky insects.

These and other emerging insects provide food for up to three billion migrating birds that have spent the cold winter months in Mexico, Central America, and South America. The returning birds include eagles, waterfowl, and songbirds. The birds come to the taiga to lay their eggs and raise their young before heading south once again when winter approaches.

Insects are not the only ones to take cover during the winter. Many small mammals, such as mice, tunnel down into the snow to keep warm. The air-filled snow is like a blanket, keeping the temperature beneath the snow just below freezing, even when it is –50°F in the air above.

However, many taiga animals tough it out, staying active through the long, bitter winter. Here are a few examples of how they survive in the frigid weather.

Gray Wolves

Gray wolves are predators. During the spring and summer months, they usually hunt alone, choosing small animals, such as squirrels and beavers, for their prey. But during the winter, these wolves are much more likely to hunt in groups, called packs. They use teamwork to track and kill large moose and caribou, and then they share the food. This change in behavior helps the wolves survive the taiga winter.

Gray wolves can run as fast as forty-five miles per hour for short distances.

Moose

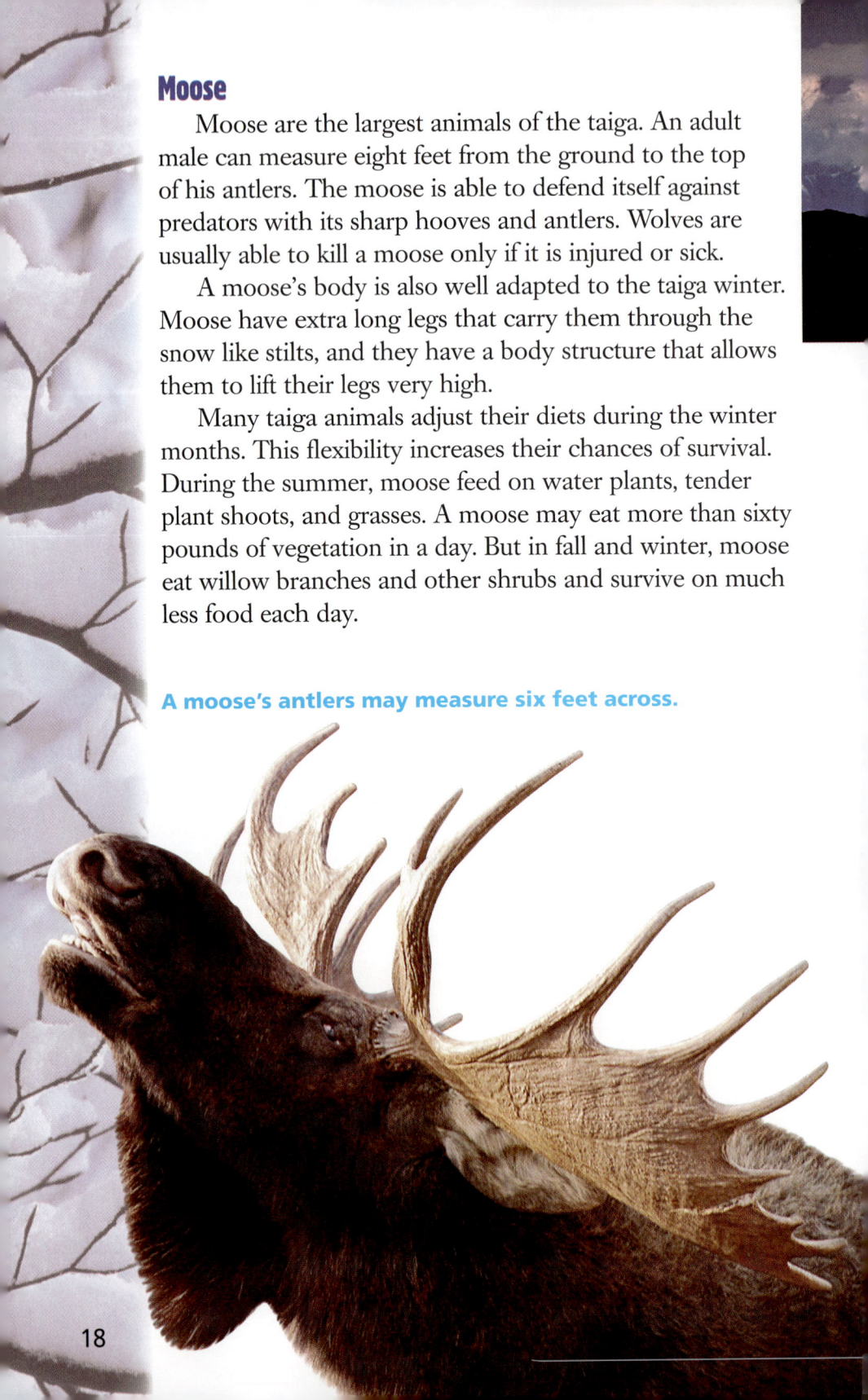

Moose are the largest animals of the taiga. An adult male can measure eight feet from the ground to the top of his antlers. The moose is able to defend itself against predators with its sharp hooves and antlers. Wolves are usually able to kill a moose only if it is injured or sick.

A moose's body is also well adapted to the taiga winter. Moose have extra long legs that carry them through the snow like stilts, and they have a body structure that allows them to lift their legs very high.

Many taiga animals adjust their diets during the winter months. This flexibility increases their chances of survival. During the summer, moose feed on water plants, tender plant shoots, and grasses. A moose may eat more than sixty pounds of vegetation in a day. But in fall and winter, moose eat willow branches and other shrubs and survive on much less food each day.

A moose's antlers may measure six feet across.

Caribou

Caribou have large, wide hooves that act like snowshoes on ice and snow. Wolves often try to chase caribou onto frozen lakes, where they may slip and fall. Because of this, caribou, moose, and other deer avoid being chased onto ice by wolves. Instead, they run away from the ice to outdistance the wolf pack and escape. Caribou are also helped through the cold months by a very well-insulated coat. The individual hairs are shaped to trap warm air next to the caribou's skin.

Caribou are also called reindeer.

Porcupines

Porcupines are known for the **quills** that defend them from predators. The quills are actually **stiffened** hairs. Porcupines do not hibernate, but during severe weather they often take shelter in dens, caves, hollow logs, or trees. A thick layer of body fat helps keeps them warm. During the summer, porcupines eat tender buds and leaves of birch, aspen, and willow trees, but in winter they are able to make do with the inner bark of conifers.

A porcupine has about thirty thousand quills.

A bobcat chases a snowshoe hare.

Snowshoe Hares

Almost every predator in the taiga pursues the snowshoe hare, but several adaptations help this animal escape. The snowshoe hare can spread its toes so that its feet are as wide as a wolf's. In winter, extra fur grows on the hare's feet and between its toes. With these "snowshoes," a hare can move quickly over the snow. The fur of the snowshoe hare changes colors with the seasons—brown in summer, spotted in spring and fall, and white in winter. This camouflage helps hide the hare from its many predators.

Crossbills

The crossbill, a type of finch, is able to survive the taiga winter because of its special beak. The top and the bottom do not meet in the middle, but cross. It may look awkward, but it is perfect for the **painstaking** work of getting conifer seeds out of their tough cones. This feature provides the crossbill with a year-round food supply.

A crossbill's beak is adapted for getting seeds from cones.

Chapter 6 The People of the Taiga

Humans have lived in the taiga forests of Europe and Asia for more than forty thousand years. When they first arrived, they lived by hunting and fishing. Some still do. Many of these people were nomadic, moving from place to place as the seasons changed. A few thousand years ago, some taiga people began to raise herds of reindeer. The Sami people of Scandinavia still make their living this way.

The taiga forests of North America were settled much later. It may have been only twelve thousand years ago that people moved into this region. Over time, these settlers occupied every part of the taiga forest. They too lived by hunting and fishing, as some still do today.

The traditional people of the taiga forests discovered ways to cope with the harsh winters. For example, they invented snowshoes to walk on the soft, deep snow. In Canada they perfected the toboggan, a long sled made of wood, and in Scandinavia they invented a ten-foot-long sled to be pulled by a domesticated reindeer. Inhabitants of the taiga also developed a type of snow shelter, called a *quinzhee*, which is a shelter dug out of a mound of snow.

Snowshoes are needed for walking on soft, deep taiga snow.

Because of the harsh conditions in the taiga, the population has grown slowly. A few hundred years ago, Russians began to migrate into the Siberian taiga. They built small villages and started farms. In the late 1700s, Europeans began to colonize the areas that are now Canada and Alaska. The demand for fur brought many trappers to the taiga in search of foxes, minks, sables, and beavers.

Today, millions of people live in the taiga regions of North America, Europe, and Asia. Some of these people are descendants of the original settlers. Many continue to lead a nomadic way of life, by hunting, fishing, and practicing traditional arts and customs. Some people live in remote villages that can be reached only by plane or by water, but most live in larger communities built up around industries that support the people, such as mining, forestry, and fishing.

Because of its severe climate and harsh living conditions, much of the taiga has remained wild, untamed, and unspoiled. But the taiga regions of the world contain many valuable natural resources, including timber, minerals, coal, oil, natural gas, water for hydroelectric power, diamonds, gold, and furs. Some people are concerned that the taiga biome could be reduced in size. Certain types of logging might damage the forest, as well as the plants and animals that live there. Roads and railroads that carry workers and equipment into the taiga, and resources back out, can threaten natural habitats. Mining operations could pollute the water, air, and land.

The people who live in the taiga are looking for ways to support themselves and their families while protecting the taiga at the same time.

Some taiga people still herd reindeer to support their families.

Glossary

hatchet *n.* a small ax with a short handle, for use with one hand.

ignites *v.* sets on fire.

painstaking *adj.* very careful; particular; diligent.

quills *n.* stiff, sharp hairs or spines like the pointed end of a feather.

registers *v.* is recorded; indicates.

smoldered *v.* burned and smoked without flame.

stiffened *v.* made or became rigid, fixed.